The Waterman/Harewood Piano Series

Piano Playtime Book Two

First solos and duets
written, selected and edited by

Fanny Waterman

and

Marion Harewood

Faber Music Limited

London

©1978 by Faber Music Ltd
First published in 1978 by Faber Music Ltd
3 Queen Square, London WC1N 3AU
Music drawn by Michael Terry
Illustrations by Anne Shingleton
Cover design by Shirley Tucker
Printed in England by Halstan & Co Ltd

Contents

The editors offer grateful thanks to Jonathan Dunsby and Paul de Keyser for their compositions included in this volume.

1 Lavender's Blue

Arr. F. W.

2 Round and Round

Carl CZERNY
(1791–1857)

3 **Autumn Leaves**

P. de K.

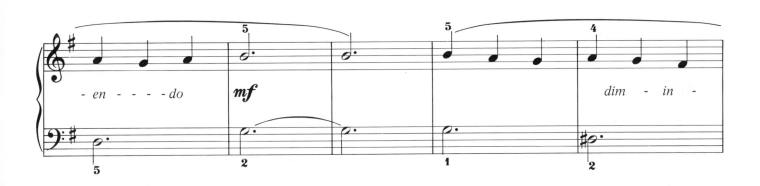

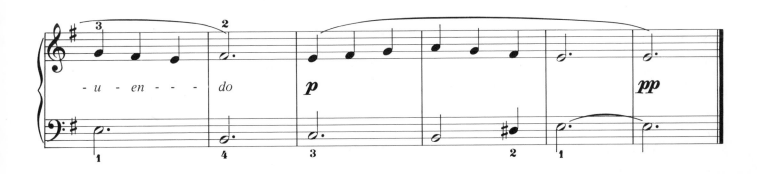

4 Campdown Races

Stephen FOSTER

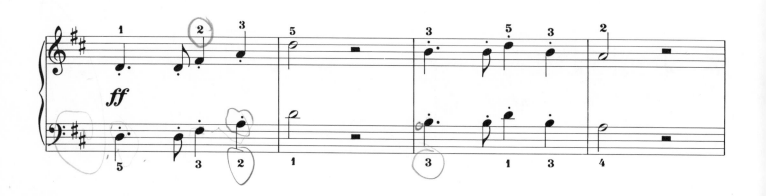

5 Cat and Mouse

F.W.

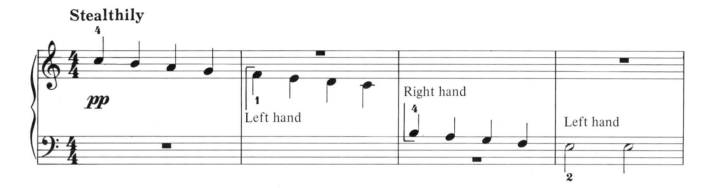

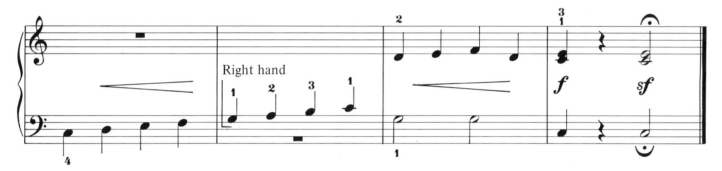

6 Sailing Along

F.W.

7 **Sleep, Little One, Sleep**

German Lullaby
arr. F. W.

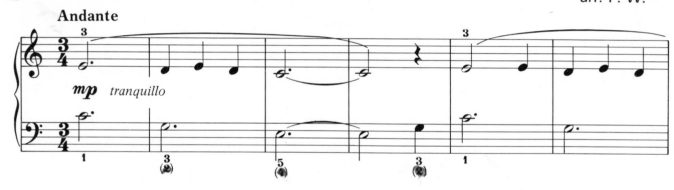

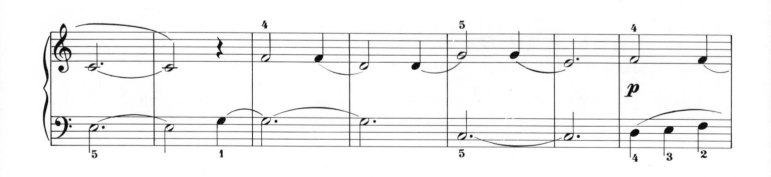

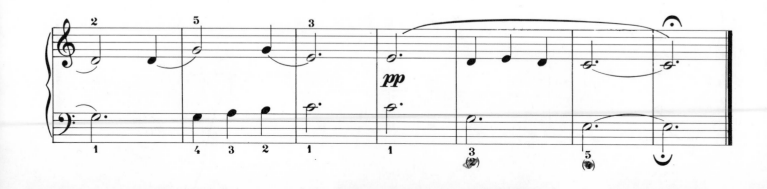

8 The Organ Grinder

Isidore PHILIPP

9 **Jingle Bells**

Arr. F. W.

This piece can also be played an octave higher (both hands)

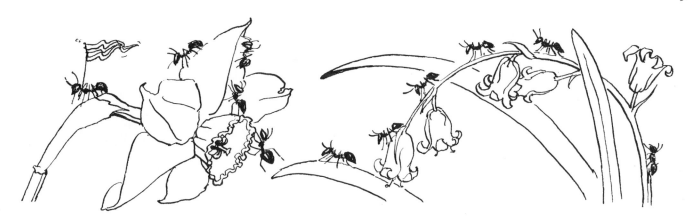

9

10 Follow my Leader

J. D.

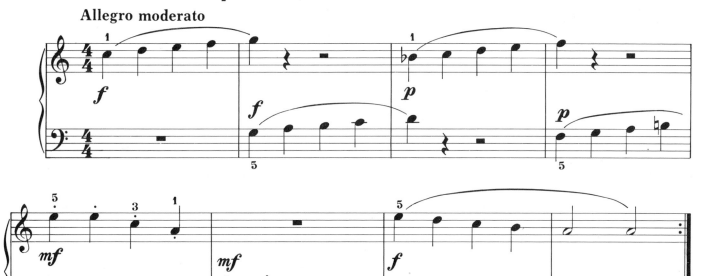

11 Sing a Song of Happiness

F.W.

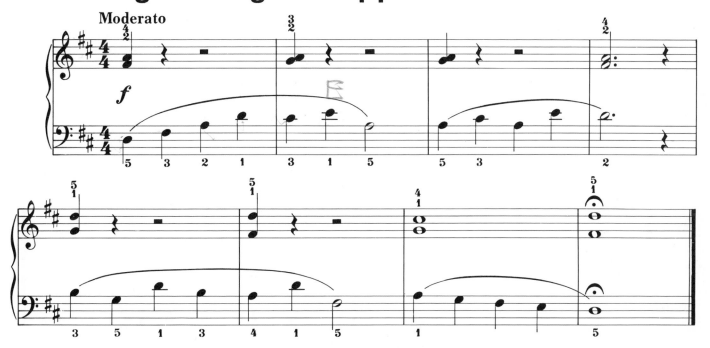

12 Pitter Patter Raindrops

F.W.

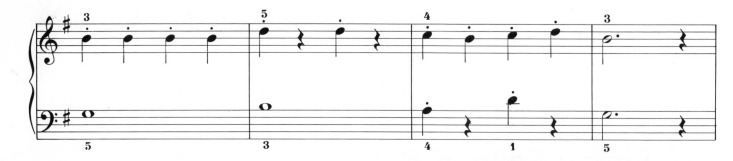

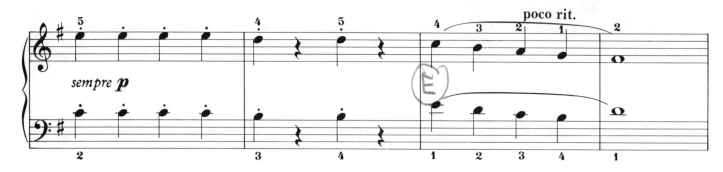

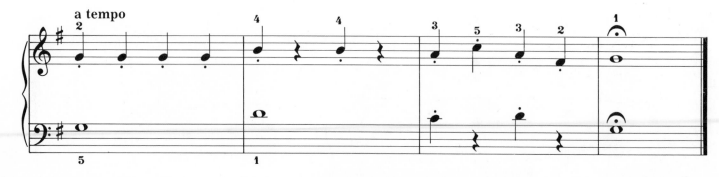

13 Bee's Birthday

F.W.

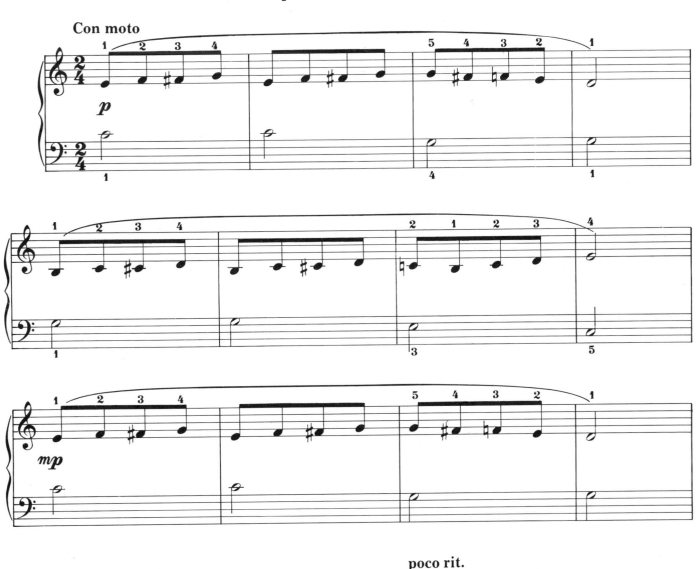

14   Mee-ow

J. D.

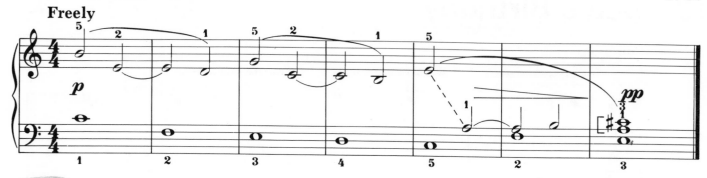

15   The Woodpecker

F. W.

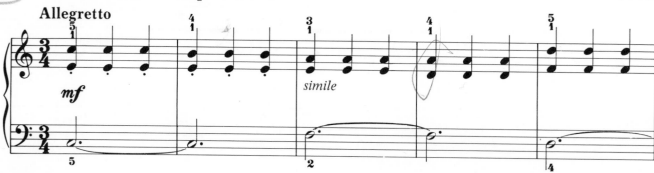

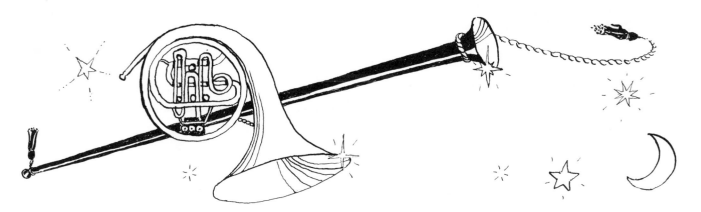

16 Magic Horns

J. D.

17 Come and Play

F. W.

18 Sunshine

Josef GRUBER

Secondo

18 Sunshine

Josef GRUBER

Primo

19 Happy and Sad

Josef GRUBER

Secondo

19 Happy and Sad

Josef GRUBER

Allegretto   **Primo**

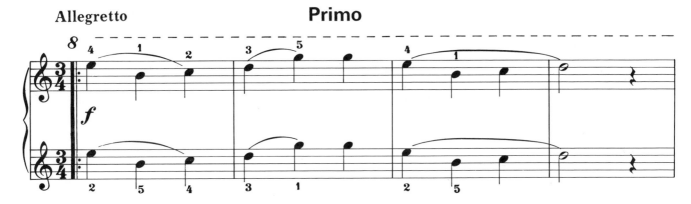

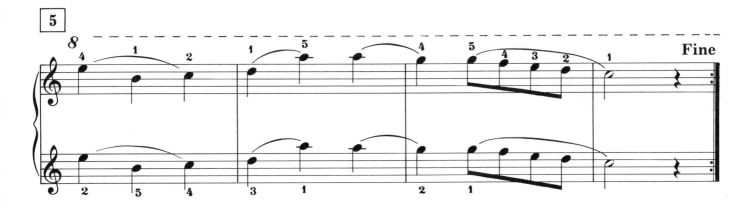

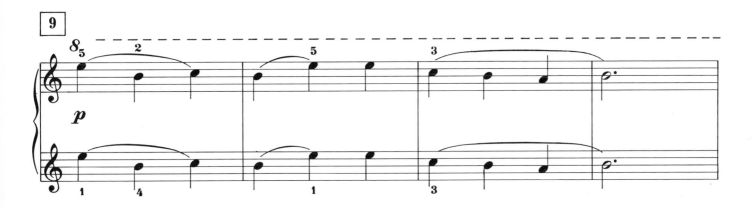

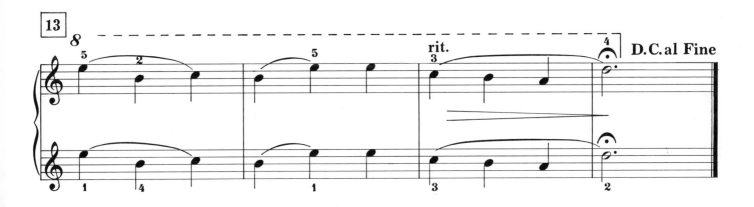

20 Waltz

Josef GRUBER

Secondo

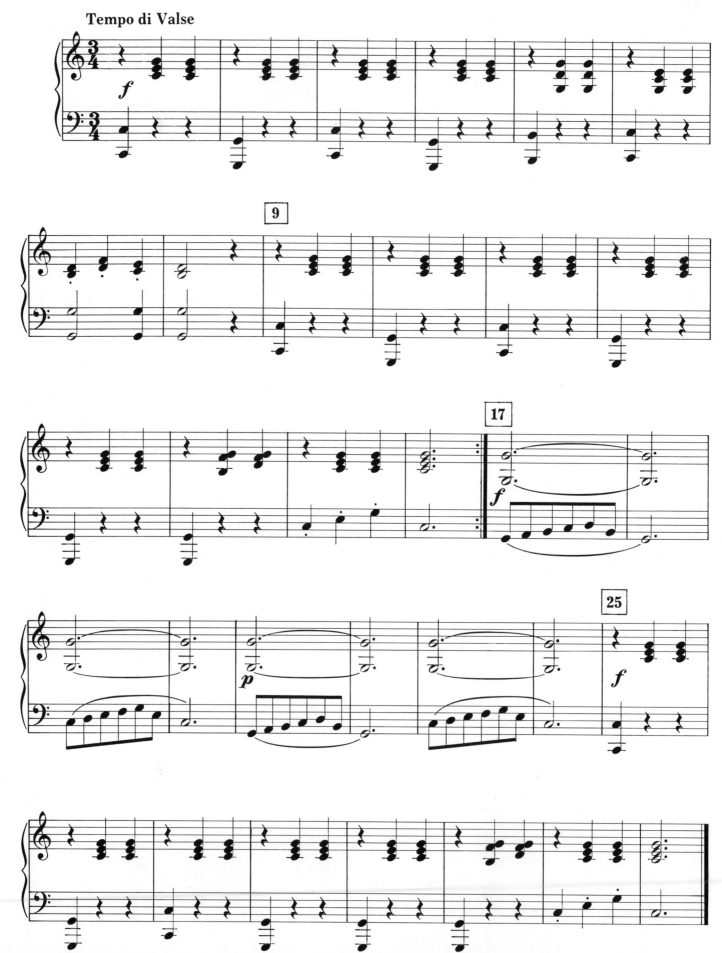

20 Waltz

Josef GRUBER

Primo

21 Little John

Josef GRUBER

Secondo

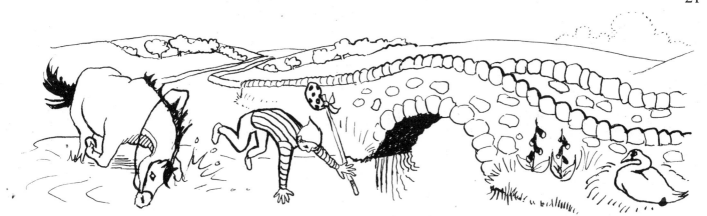

21 Little John

Josef GRUBER

Primo

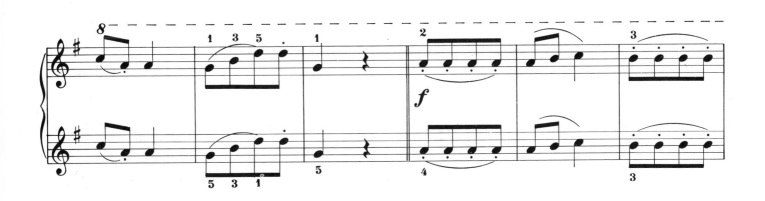

22 Pierrot

Secondo